# DISCOVER
# Medical Chemistry

MW01520692

by Libby Romero

## Table of Contents

# Introduction

People use **chemistry**. People use **medical** chemistry.

▲ People use chemistry in medicine.

# Words to Know

chemistry

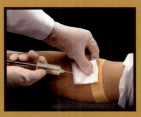

disease

matter

medical

nutritionists

pharmacists

See the Glossary on page 22.

3

# What Is Chemistry?

Chemistry is a type of science.

▲ Chemistry is science.

Chemistry is about **matter**.

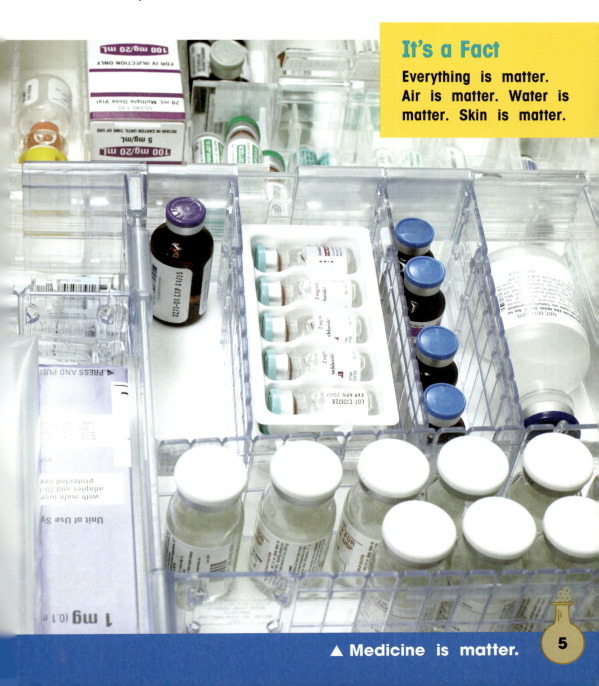

▲ Medicine is matter.

Chemistry is about how matter changes.

▲ **Chemistry is about matter.**

Chemistry is about how matter combines.

**Figure It Out**

Look around you. What matter do you see? How does that matter change?

▲ Chemistry is about matter.

# Why Do People Need Medical Chemistry?

Medical chemistry helps people.

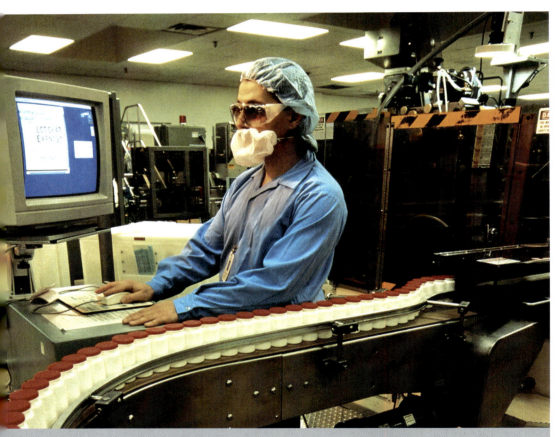

▲ People need chemistry to make medicines.

## Did You Know?

People make some medicines from trees.

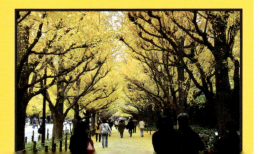

Medical chemistry helps doctors. Medical chemistry helps doctors fight **disease**.

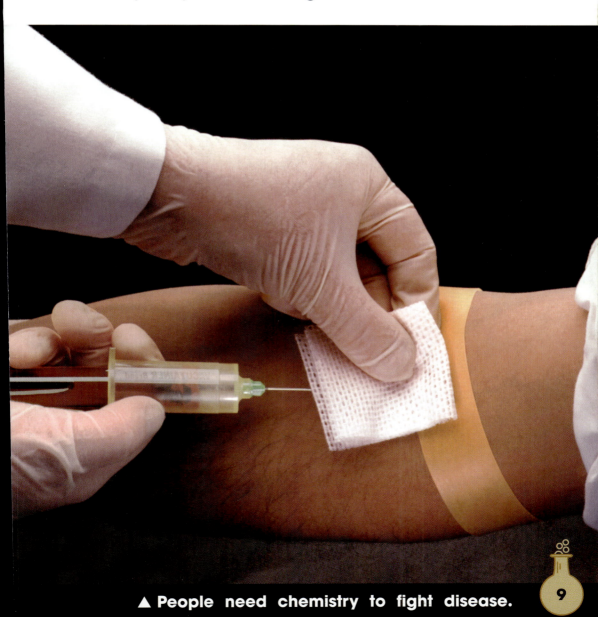

▲ **People need chemistry to fight disease.**

Medical chemistry helps sick people. Medical chemistry helps patients.

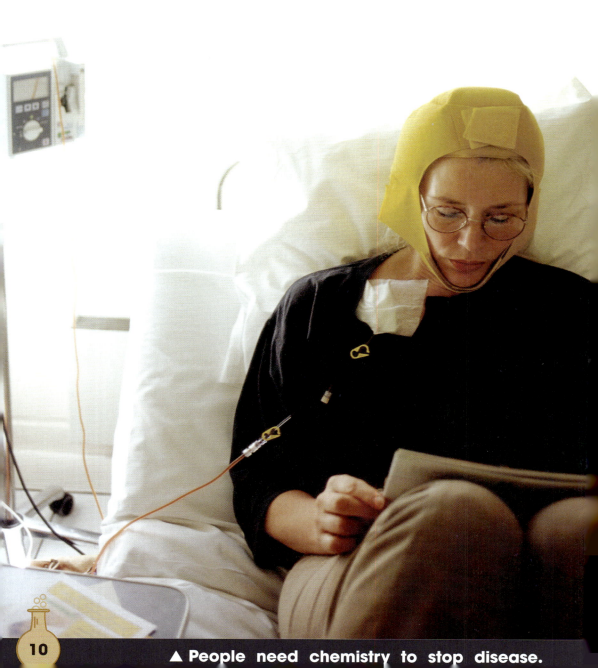

▲ People need chemistry to stop disease.

Medical chemistry helps animals.

▲ **People need chemistry to help animals.**

# Who Uses Medical Chemistry?

Many people use medical chemistry.

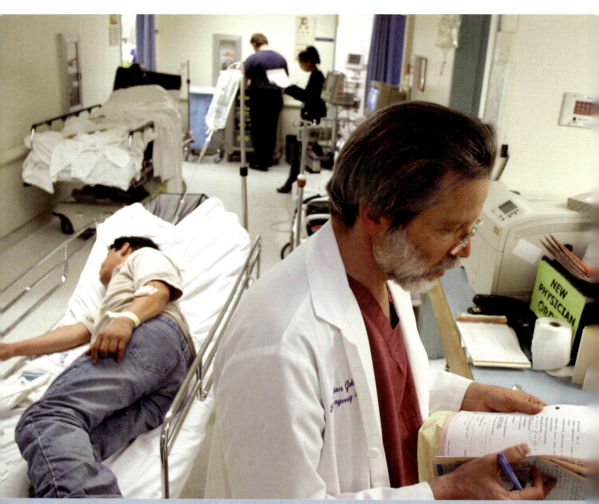

▲ People know about medical chemistry.

Scientists use medical chemistry.

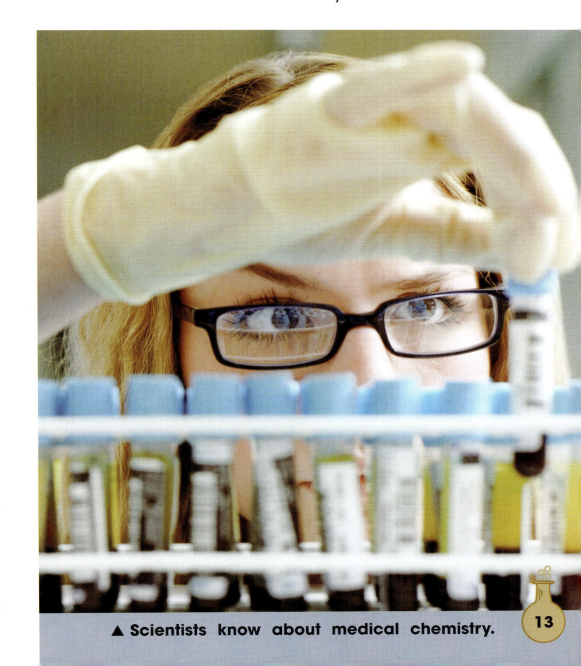

▲ Scientists know about medical chemistry.

Doctors use medical chemistry.

▲ **Doctors know about medical chemistry.**

## It's a Fact

**Doctors find diseases in blood. Doctors find diseases on skin. Doctors find diseases in the heart.**

**Nutritionists** use medical chemistry.

▲ Nutritionists know about medical chemistry.

**Pharmacists** use medical chemistry. Pharmacists use medical chemistry every day.

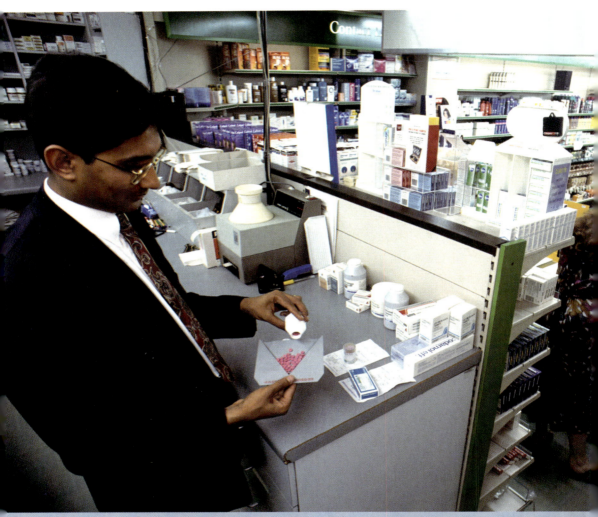

▲ **Pharmacists know about medical chemistry.**

## Did You Know?

**Doctors are scientists. Nutritionists are scientists. Pharmacists are scientists, too.**

People use medical chemistry every day.

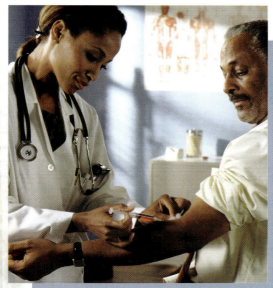

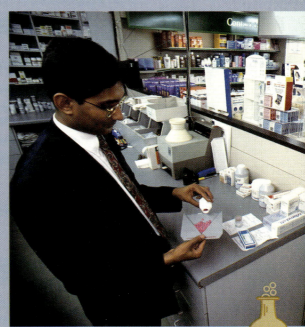

▲ Many people know about medical chemistry.

# Conclusion

Medical chemistry helps people.

▲ People use medical chemistry.

# Concept Map

## Medical Chemistry

### What Is Chemistry?

- a type of science
- about matter
- about how matter changes
- about how matter combines

### Why Do People Need Medical Chemistry?

- helps people
- helps doctors fight disease
- helps sick people
- helps patients
- helps animals

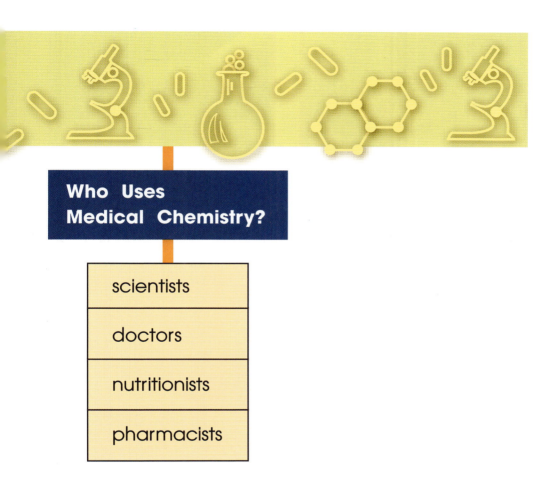

**Who Uses Medical Chemistry?**

| |
|---|
| scientists |
| doctors |
| nutritionists |
| pharmacists |

# Glossary

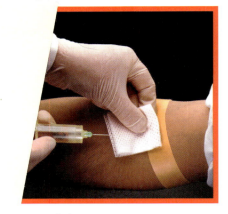

**ase** sickness

**Chemistry** is abo...

...dical chemistry helps doctors ...t **disease**.

**matter** something that occupies space

*Chemistry is about **matter**.*

**medical** about the practice of medicine

*People use **medical** chemistry.*

22

**nutritionists** scientists who teach about food

*Nutritionists use medical chemistry.*

**pharmacists** scientists who sell medicines

*Pharmacists use medical chemistry.*

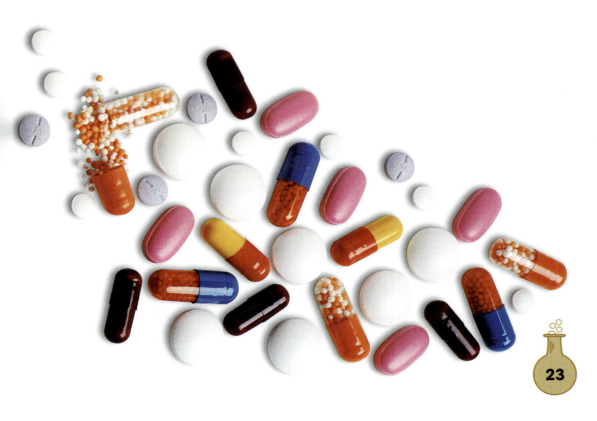

# Index

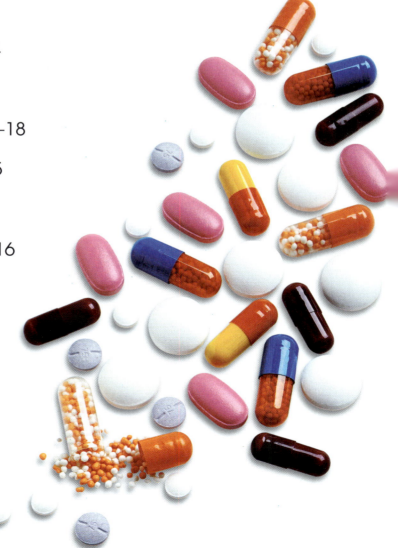